A special gift for

_____

From

_____

Date

_____

OUR PURPOSE AT HOWARD PUBLISHING IS TO:

- *Increase faith* in the hearts of growing Christians
- *Inspire holiness* in the lives of believers
- *Instill hope* in the hearts of struggling people everywhere

BECAUSE HE'S COMING AGAIN!

Holding the World by the Hand © 2005 by Gigi Schweikert
All rights reserved. Printed in the United States of America
Published by Howard Publishing Co., Inc.
3117 North 7th Street, West Monroe, Louisiana 71291-2227
www.howardpublishing.com

05 06 07 08 09 10 11 12 13 14   10 9 8 7 6 5 4 3 2 1

Edited by Between the Lines
Cover design LinDee Loveland
Interior design by Tennille Paden

Library of Congress Cataloging-in-Publication Data

Schweikert, Gigi 1962–
  Holding the world by the hand / Gigi Schweikert.
      p. cm.
  ISBN 1-58229-418-6
    1. Mother and child—Religious aspects—Christianity. 2. Mothers—Religious life. I. Title.

  BV4529.18.S39 2005
  248.8'431—dc22

                                                              2004059691

Holding the World by the Hand

Gigi Schweikert

Contents

A Note to All Who H

A Note to All Who Hold the World by the Hand

When you hold the hand of your child in yours, you are holding the future of the world. For wrapped inside your child are the hopes and dreams of lifetimes to come. No matter that you sometimes don't feel up to the task—God has placed within you a heart made for love and a soul created for caring. From generation to generation the seeds of creativity, possibility, and potential are passed through a mother's hand to an expectant world.

In this little book, you will find simple directives, sweet stories, and eternal truths that will help you impart to your child the qualities that shape the world—qualities like confidence, faith, generosity, hope, laughter, and love.

Your touch, your embrace, your kiss—these are the instruments that define the world of your child. As you stoop to kiss and embrace to comfort and reach to help your child, you are kissing and comforting and helping the whole world.

A mother changes th

CHAPTER ONE

Affection

A mother
changes the
world, one kiss
at a time.

The world is always changing. Many of these changes inspire trust and fill us with reassurance. Others bring uncertainty and fear.

Sometimes, even as mothers, we question the importance of our role. Yet we have been blessed with the greatest work of all. God has given us the power to offer comfort, love, and laughter. Mothers are making a tremendous difference in countless little lives. We are changing the world, one kiss at a time.

Kiss your child
affectionately
and say,
"I am blessed
to be your mother."

The Daydream

"Mom," my son called from downstairs.

"I'm upstairs," I shouted back.

"Do you know where my sneakers are?"

"Under the chair in the kitchen."

Not two seconds had gone by when I heard, "Mom, do you know where my skates are?"

I called out, "In the garage, on the shelf." How was he planning to wear sneakers and skates at the same time? "Please don't yell up again," I added. As I turned to the laundry on my bed, he appeared at my bedroom door.

"Do you—," he began, but I stopped him.

"Why are you asking me where all your things are?"

"Because you know where everything is," he responded.

I wasn't sure if that was a compliment or a newly added responsibility in the official mommy job description. Either way, I did know where most things were.

I used to envision motherhood as my children and I in matching white linen clothes, frolicking in the backyard with bunnies or puppies or some small animal, and gathering flowers and organic vegetables from our garden.

Now in the throes of parenting and moving at mommy hyperspeed, I realized that we didn't even own matching towels, let alone matching outfits, and that the only things I harvested were socks from the dryer that needed matching. I stood before my laundry basket feeling sorry for myself.

The hardest part about being a mom is the constant necessity to serve others and to meet their needs. I enjoy giving my son nutritional meals and warm hugs, clean clothes and many kisses, mommy advice and unconditional love. But am I really making a difference?

Before becoming a mom, I used to have business cards with my name on them. If I had some now, they would simply read "Child's Mom." Not a bad identity, considering how wonderful my child is and how much I love being his mother. But somehow between calling out spelling words in the car and waging the never-ending battle against grass stains, I longed for that imaginary business card to at least read "Child's Mom, Vice-President of Mothering." I wanted to be recognized for the best Jell-O mold at the preschool party. I wanted to be given a glowing performance appraisal indicating my exemplary record of handing in Boy Scout candy proceeds and field-trip permission slips on time—usually early.

In fact, what I really wanted was a promotion: "Child's Mom, President of Mothering," awarded to me for baking all those extra cupcakes, putting in overtime during long nights when my son was sick, and selling the most rolls of wrapping paper for the school fund-raiser.

"Mom?" I heard my son call just as I was about to receive my scepter. Snapping back from my daydream, I asked, "What do you need?"

"Nothing. I just wanted to tell you that you do a lot of cool stuff, like making my clothes smell good and cooking yummy food and knowing where my skates are." As he flopped onto my bed, he added, "I love you, Mommy."

At that moment I realized that my mommy dreams really had come true. I am president of mothering in my son's eyes. And I don't need a business card to prove it.

Write the story of one of your kisses and the effect it had on your child . . .

_____

_____

_____

_____

_____

_____

_____

_____

_____

_____

_____

_____

_____

_____

_____

_____

A mother holds her chi

CHAPTER TWO

Attachment

A mother

holds her

child's hand just

long enough.

Sometimes it's difficult to leave our children with someone else, even for a few hours. Other times we long for those quiet moments alone, free to move about unencumbered by small hands constantly tugging at us.

Although separation can be hard, children benefit from time away too, learning to comfort themselves, making new friends, and realizing that mommies always come back.

Place your hand on your child's heart and say, "Even when we're apart, we are together in our hearts."

The First Day of School

I had anticipated the first day my child would go off to preschool, ready to take on finger paint and Play-Doh. She'd be dressed in a special first-day-of-school outfit with a bright pink backpack. We'd snap pictures on the steps of the nursery school like it was her high-school prom. Before she ran off to play with her new friends, I'd kiss her good-bye, then I'd skip down the stairs to have coffee with my own friends, looking forward to all the things I could do in 120 minutes of precious me time.

Here's how it actually went. My daughter wouldn't wear the special, grandmother-purchased dress, but insisted on an ensemble of her own. The only pink item was the top she'd picked out to go with her orange pants. Instead of her backpack, she toted a blanket I was hoping the rest of the world would never see—especially her preschool teachers, who would surely determine the fate of her Ivy-League education. And the rolls of film went unused—she refused to smile or even pause for a picture.

What I didn't expect from this fiercely independent three-year-old was the reaction I got when I leaned down to kiss her good-bye. My child burst into tears, begging me not to leave her.

Everything in me wanted to scoop her up and save her from that nasty old preschool. How could I soothe her? How could I help her understand that I would always be there for her, even when she was on her own? Then I realized that our mother-child bond, the one that made her want to cling to me for dear life, was the same bond that would enable her to stand on her own.

Kneeling down and placing my hand on her rapidly beating heart, I said, "Even when we're apart, sweetie, we're together in our hearts. Every time you feel your heart beat, you can know that I'm with you." Looking at me quizzically, she placed her small hand on her heart and felt the beat. This exchange became our nursery-school drop-off ritual. We'd place our hands on our hearts and take comfort in knowing that with every beat, we could feel each other's presence.

Those preschool years quickly passed, and my daughter learned to run into class with excitement and confidence.

I'd forgotten all about our reassuring gesture until I was leaving for my first overnight trip alone. I was worried about going away and leaving my family. The children were standing outside with my husband, and we were saying our good-byes. My husband must have sensed my hesitation and tried to reassure me, "You'll be fine, honey, and we'll be fine too." Trying not to cry, I told the children, "I'll be back in a few days with a little surprise for everyone."

As I was kissing them good-bye, I noticed my oldest daughter was holding her chest with her hand. "What's the matter, sweetie—are you all right?"

"Remember what we used to do when I was in preschool?" my daughter asked. Then she placed my hand on my heart and said, "Don't worry, Mommy. Even when we're apart, we're always together in our hearts. You'll know I'm with you every time your heart beats."

On the airplane I laid my hand on my heart again, smiled, and relaxed. No matter how old you are, it's easier to venture out when you know someone is with you.

Record a time when you had to let go of your child's hand . . .

_____

_____

_____

_____

_____

_____

_____

_____

_____

_____

_____

_____

_____

_____

_____

_____

_____

A mother's eyes are op

CHAPTER THREE

Belief

A mother's

eyes are opened by

her child's belief.

$\mathcal{A}$s mothers we often get caught up in the everyday struggles of life. We rely only on the things we can see, and at times we're even blind to those.

God has filled the world with little miracles unfolding in front of us each day. Yet it often takes the eyes of our own children and the strong belief in their hearts to help us see.

Embrace your
child gratefully
and say,
"Through your
eyes, I see
miracles."

Seeds

"What's this?" my daughter asked as she sorted through the bag of free stuff I picked up during a conference.

"Those are flower seeds with special soil to grow them in," I responded matter-of-factly, trying to evenly divide the rest of the goodies among my other children. There were rulers and bookmarks, stickers and magnets, all imprinted with the logos of various organizations. I thought the stuff was a waste of time and money, and if I hadn't been searching for last-minute gifts to tote home for my kids, I would have passed on all of it.

"Can I have the flower seeds and soil?" my oldest asked. "Sure, honey." I didn't think much about her request then, but long after the chocolate bars, neon rulers, and luggage tags had lost their allure, the packet of seeds still held treasures only beginning to unfold.

"Look, Mom. God does make little miracles," my daughter told me excitedly. She pulled me over to the window sill in her bedroom to see a small pot with little sprouts appearing through the moist dirt. I never even knew she had planted the seeds. But she had patiently watered them, believing all the time that eventually they would be flowers. The sprouts grew to plants, the plants produced buds, and the buds opened into beautiful marigold blossoms. My daughter was amazed, and so was I. "Aren't they beautiful?" she asked.

"They sure are," I told her. "You did a great job, honey."

After the flowers bloomed, we forgot all about the little pot until one of the seasonal cleanups of my daughter's room. I was ready to toss the dried-up pot of flowers, container and all, into the large black bag along with the other discards of candy wrappers and half-completed coloring-book pages. But my daughter had another idea. She grabbed a dried flower head off one of the stems, and a flurry of seeds scattered on her carpet. "Look, Mom! There's a little flower in each one of these seeds."

"Are you sure you want to keep those seeds, honey?" I tried to convince her to dump them in the trash. It just seemed like a mess to me.

She collected all the flower seeds in a small sandwich

bag and put them in her dresser drawer for safekeeping.

When I began my spring planting a few months later, my daughter appeared outside, bag in hand, requesting a pot and soil. I didn't think those old seeds would even sprout, but I didn't want to dampen her enthusiasm, so I helped her with the things she needed. She planted the marigold seeds in a huge terra-cotta pot—and again the flowers grew.

Throughout the summer my daughter plucked the dried flower heads off the plant and saved the seeds. The following spring she requested a small section of the family garden for herself. She filled the entire space with flowers that just two years ago had been only one small package of seeds. "Can you believe all these flowers came from just a few seeds?" she marveled. "They're little miracles."

Oh yes. I believed.

What miracle have you seen through your child's eyes? . . .

_____

_____

_____

_____

_____

_____

_____

_____

_____

_____

_____

_____

_____

_____

_____

_____

_____

_____

A mother's pres

CHAPTER FOUR

Calmness

A mother's presence calms her child.

The world moves so quickly. There are ballet lessons and school lessons, field trips and grocery trips. And as mothers we sometimes forget to "hop off" with our children and spend time enjoying calm, simple moments with them.

Our children need to spend unrushed, relaxed time with us. We can't stop the world from turning, but we can create a calm and peaceful home, a retreat from the everyday, a place where hearts can be heard.

Touch your
child gently
and say,
"Enjoy the simple,
calm moments
in life."

Making Lemonade

"It's time for soccer. Grab your shoes and let's get in the car," I called to my son. He was lying on his side on the floor, moving small action figures in various scenarios of distress and rescue. I felt like I was the one in distress. I was always saying things like "We're going to be late for baseball." "Hurry up." "You have drum lessons in ten minutes."

As I stood watching him play, I realized he didn't seem stressed at all. On the contrary, my son looked thoroughly content making action noises to accompany his fictitious dramatic adventures. I was about to yell "Let's go" for the final time. But for some reason I didn't. "How about we just hang out at home this afternoon and do stuff around here?" I asked, not sure what his reaction would be.

"Really, Mom?" he glanced up with excitement.

"Sure."

He resumed playing, and I proceeded to the kitchen to have a cup of coffee and look through the mail. The house was quiet and peaceful.

Later that afternoon my son and I journeyed outside to kick his soccer ball around. We scored points by kicking the ball into our makeshift goal of rocks and sticks. He won. When the game was over, we collapsed in the grass and watched the clouds go by. Then we marveled at an ant carrying a piece of potato chip twice its size.

"How about something cold to drink?" I asked. We pulled ourselves up off the grass and headed inside. "Lemonade good?" I inquired.

"OK, Mom." He headed to the pantry to grab some lemonade mix.

"Let's make real lemonade," I suggested.

"How do you do that?" he replied.

"Well, it takes some skill. Are you up for the challenge?"

I showed him all about choosing just the right lemons, rolling them before you cut them, and juicing them with the crystal hand juicer. My son put in the sugar, a bit much, yet somehow perfect for the sweetness of the day. He stirred the concoction, and we poured our homemade lemonade into glasses full of ice. Then I kissed him on the head, and we headed to the porch. After counting the seeds at the bottom of our glasses, we decided we'd grow our own lemon tree one day.

That night as I tucked my son into bed, he reached up and said, "Thanks, Mom."

"For what, sweetie?"

"For the best day ever."

Tell the story of a slow day spent with your child . . .

_____

_____

_____

_____

_____

_____

_____

_____

_____

_____

_____

_____

_____

_____

_____

_____

A mother's arms are th

CHAPTER FIVE

Comfort

A mother's
arms are the perfect
cradle in which to comfort
her child.

There's something beautifully rhythmic about the rocking motion of a mother comforting her baby. We soothe our overtired children with soft caresses and heal skinned knees with kisses.

Sometimes, when our children experience loss or uncertainty, we feel unsure how to console them. But whether our children are infants or adults, the greatest comfort we can give is our presence and our warm embrace.

Hold your child securely in your arms and say, "I will always be here to comfort you."

Stars

The son of one of my good friends died unexpectedly at the age of seven. I wasn't sure what to say or do for my friend. I went to her home and stayed with her that night.

It was a cold, clear evening, and from their home high upon the hill, you could see the star-filled sky. Her son's telescope was perched facing skyward on the front deck. It was strange to see it standing alone, without the young boy peering through the lens to the vast heavens. He loved stars.

My friend had cared for my older children when they were babies. Her son and my children had been more than friends. They were like siblings. When I told my seven-year-old daughter that her friend had died, she responded with tears and with questions I could hardly answer.

"Why?"

"His heart just stopped, honey."

"Where is he now?"

"He's in heaven."

"How did he get to heaven?"

"God took him, sweetie."

When I told my other child, who was five, about the death, she simply asked, "When is he coming back?"

"He's not, honey."

All I could do to help my children was to hold them, be with them, and let them begin, slowly, to accept what had happened.

My husband and I decided not to take our children to the funeral because they were so young. On the day of the memorial service, my daughter handed me a crayon-colored card secured tightly with wrinkled strips of tape. "Give this to my friend," she said. I wondered what was inside.

The church was full. More than five hundred people had come to show love and support for this wonderful family. I placed the card in the casket with my friend's son.

We returned from the service to find the children very sad. "We didn't get a chance to say good-bye to our friend," they cried. They were right. I hadn't thought about that.

"He wasn't at the funeral," I tried to explain. "He's in heaven." But I realized that they needed some closure, so I promised, "You'll get a chance to say good-bye."

That night I bundled up the kids and we drove to the observatory where their friend liked to spend time with his dad. It was late on a weeknight, and the observatory was vacant. I gathered one child on each side of me and held them close. For every star we saw, we yelled, "Good-bye!"

When our farewells were done and the children were resting silently in my arms, I told my older daughter, "I gave your friend your card."

She looked satisfied and said, "Good. God will read it to him."

Death is the greatest loss we can experience. After fours years, my children still talk about their friend and how they miss him. And on nights when the sky is clear, we still go outside and shout to the stars.

Write the story of a time you comforted your child . . .

_____

_____

_____

_____

_____

_____

_____

_____

_____

_____

_____

_____

_____

_____

_____

_____

_____

_____

A mother knows

CHAPTER SIX

Confidence

A mother

knows her child

is special.

At times we wish we were prettier, smarter, or wealthier. Sometimes mothers even wish such things for their children. But we don't really want to change them.

We know each child is special and that if children are confident in themselves, they won't envy someone else. Mothers understand that the greatest wealth is knowing what you have to offer and doing it in your own special way.

Whisper in your
child's ear,
"You can do
great things
by just
being yourself."

The Hair Stylist

From the time she was three years old, my daughter loved playing with makeup and hair accessories. By age nine she was assessing my clothes before I headed to a business meeting or special dinner.

In high school my daughter wanted to take beautician courses. Concerned for her future, I insisted, "Take the hard classes in school so you can get into a good college. Then, in the afternoons, you can work a few hours at a salon." Everyone at the salon loved her. She wasn't allowed to cut hair at the shop because she didn't have a license, so she turned our basement into a refuge for teens with unmanageable hair. I was sure it was just a matter of time before some mom would call. "What did your daughter do to my kid's hair?" On the contrary, however, the calls I received were messages of thanks and compliments. My daughter had given those young women greater self-confidence just by helping them be more stylish.

When it was time for college, I wanted my child to become a doctor. She was intelligent, good with people, and tenacious—the perfect attributes. One evening she timidly suggested that she skip college and get her license to cut hair. "But don't you want to be in a profession where you can help people?"

"But I will help people," she insisted. I completely dismissed the idea.

She was accepted at the college of my choice and spent one year there before informing my husband and me that she was dropping out and enrolling in a school for hair professionals. My husband and I were horrified. "She'll never make any money." "She's throwing her life away." She finished her training with highest honors, went to work for a successful salon in New York City, and eventually opened her own shop.

Many years later my daughter's friend from high school was diagnosed with cancer. She was facing surgery and then chemotherapy. Like most female cancer patients, the thought of losing her hair was almost as devastating as the prognosis of cancer.

My daughter's heart ached for her friend. Human

hair wigs were extremely expensive, but she found two at a reasonable price from a wholesaler and was able to dye and cut the wigs to perfectly match her friend's hair color and style. She created a slightly modified do with the second wig for variety. I was there when she presented her friend with the wigs. We all cried as my daughter lovingly and gently fitted the first one on her friend's head.

I caught my daughter's eye in the mirror. She turned to me with the confidence and contentment of a young woman comfortable with herself and her place in the world. "See, Mom, doesn't she look great?" The expression on her friend's face spoke volumes. *Oh.* I almost gasped audibly. Suddenly it was clear. My daughter had been helping others in her own way since she was a teenager. I just hadn't been able to see it.

"Beautiful, honey," I said. "What you do is amazing."

Tell about a time your child affected a person by using his or her God-given gifts . . .

_____

_____

_____

_____

_____

_____

_____

_____

_____

_____

_____

_____

_____

_____

_____

_____

A mother's gentle wo

CHAPTER SEVEN

Encouragement

A mother's

gentle words

encourage

her child.

A mother's loving, encouraging words give her children strength. As they feel their way through the world, overstepping here, unsure there, our support helps them develop a positive attitude, a willingness to work hard, and a determination to overcome even life's biggest obstacles.

When we walk through times of uncertainty with our children, they will learn that they have the power to be successful.

Lay your hands firmly on your child's shoulders and say, "You can do it."

The Spelling Bee

As I was tucking my first-grader into bed, she said, "I have just one more question." Those are the times I want to say, "Tomorrow," because inevitably she'll ask something like "Can I have ice cream for breakfast?" or "Shouldn't I brush my teeth twice?" But I listened with something short of patience, longing for an easy chair and the stack of magazines I wanted to peruse.

"Do you ever feel worried about things, Mommy?"

"Sure, honey."

"Like what?"

"All kinds of things," I told her. "I worry about little stuff like when we have lots of people over for dinner and I want them to have a good time. And I worry about big stuff like whether I'm being a good mommy." She hugged me and assured me I was a good mother. I smiled. At least that was one thing I could cross off the list.

Sensing she must be upset about something, I tried to act like I was just starting a casual conversation. "So how was school today?" I half expected her to reply, "You already asked me that when I got home."

Instead, she confessed. "I'm not a good speller."

"You're a great speller, honey. You always do well on your spelling tests. Why do you say that?"

She lay quietly for a moment, then it all tumbled out without any breaths in between. "There's a spelling bee next week and all the kids in the class are smarter than me. I don't want to go on stage, and spelling is dumb anyway because you can just use spell-check on the computer."

I suppressed a smile and held her hand. "Are you worried about going on stage?" She started to cry, and I leaned over to give her a reassuring hug. "How about if I help you?" My daughter nodded, and we kept talking until we had a conquer-the-spelling-bee plan. We decided to study the word list every night and have a pretend spelling bee. We also created our own secret sign that she could use on stage. If she got worried, she would smile, and I would smile back to assure her.

She studied all week, and the big day arrived. "You'll be great, sweetie. Just do your best and smile if you get worried, and I'll smile back." She smiled like a beauty queen throughout the entire spelling bee. I was sure her lips wouldn't be able to move when it was her turn to spell, but she got through it just fine. She came in eighth, but she learned much more than how to spell—which was good, since she went out on the word *sang*.

She was so excited after the spelling bee that she ran up to me, holding her participation ribbon as if it were the Nobel prize. "Mommy, look!"

"I knew you could do it," I said proudly. "Were you nervous?"

"A little at first, but when I saw you smiling at me in the audience, I was OK. Just seeing you there made me feel better."

"But you were smiling the whole time," I said, a bit confused.

"Yeah," she answered nonchalantly. "That's because I didn't want you to be nervous since you're worried about being a good mommy and all."

Write about a difficult time and how you walked your child through it . . .

_____

_____

_____

_____

_____

_____

_____

_____

_____

_____

_____

_____

_____

_____

_____

_____

_____

mother has faith th

CHAPTER EIGHT

Faith

A mother

has faith that

God is with

her child.

There are times when we all fear. But as mothers we have to push through our own insecurities and step out in faith to help our children. They long for our touch, especially when they're frightened.

God works through every mother to reassure and protect her children. But even when we can't be there, our children are never alone. God is watching over them.

*Hold your
child's face
lovingly and say,
"Above all,
have faith in God."*

Icing on the Cake

When my daughter was six years old, she went through a phase of being really afraid. She didn't want to be alone. She wouldn't even venture downstairs unless someone was with her. She preferred me as her companion, but when she needed something in another part of the house and I was busy, she'd ask her older sister to accompany her. She'd beg her younger sister if she had to or even drag the baby along if she was desperate. She just wanted the comfort of having someone with her. "Stay with me, Mommy. Don't leave me alone," she'd say.

Initially I felt compassion for her. I remembered my own childhood fears, and I knew how terrifying they could be. So she became my little shadow. But after several days of having her constantly at my side, I longed for some solitude.

Every night before bed, we checked for monsters and bears—under her bed, in her closet, even in each of her dresser drawers in case there were miniature monsters and itty-bitty bears—but she was still scared. At the library, we checked out books about not being afraid, but she still was. We developed a special Fears Be Gone spray that she could carry around with her in case of emergencies. She was still frightened.

One night I could hear my daughters in the kitchen pondering why a birthday cake had cake at all when the icing was obviously the best part. "They should just make cakes out of icing," one said. The others quickly agreed. Then my oldest child went upstairs, and the youngest was on her way when the middle one anxiously pleaded, "Hey, wait for me. I don't want to be down here alone."

The four-year-old responded without hesitation, "Don't be scared, God is with you."

"You're right," I heard my six-year-old say. She sat back down and continued licking icing off her cupcake. For the first time in ages, she remained in the kitchen alone.

That evening before tucking her into bed, I started our nightly monster-and-bear check. I stooped to look under the bed, announced, "No monsters or bears here," and turned toward the closet.

"That's OK, Mommy. I'm not scared anymore."

"That's great, darling," I replied with surprise. I smoothed her covers and kissed her head. I didn't ask her about the sudden change, fearing too much discussion might make her reconsider.

As I left her room, I could hear her small voice. "God, my mommy just left, so I'm counting on You to stay with me until I fall asleep." He's been watching over her ever since.

Record a time when your child's faith stepped out on its own . . .

_____

_____

_____

_____

_____

_____

_____

_____

_____

_____

_____

_____

_____

_____

_____

_____

A mother knows frie

CHAPTER NINE

Friendship

A mother knows friendship renews her spirit.

As rewarding as motherhood can be, it also can make us long for uninterrupted showers, quiet walks, and time with other adults. We often feel isolated from other grownups, surrounded constantly by the chatter of children. We fall into a pattern of always giving to our children without ever renewing ourselves.

Sharing moments with good friends can help us renew our spirit—and it teaches our children the value of friendship.

Lay your hand
on your child's
face and say,
"Be a good friend
to others."

Mommy Friends

I called them my grown-up mommy girlfriends. These special women were bound together by a simple and easily identifiable bond—they all had children. Before motherhood, we had faced the working world with intelligence, eagerness, and drive. We'd had freshly coiffed hair, coordinated outfits, and leisure time. My friends were business owners, managers, and lawyers who had traded in their daily planners for birthday-party planners and their trips to the airport for trips to the zoo.

These were the women who kept me sane. My grown-up mommy girlfriends let me drop off my kids at their house when I had a doctor's appointment, the baby-sitter bailed, or I just needed a break. They knew when I was about to cry, when I couldn't take the crying of my children anymore, and the best movies to watch for a good cry. When I was coming unraveled, they gave me extra diapers so I didn't have to run to the store. They offered encouragement as I headed to my first parent-teacher conference . . . and after.

For some reason, they were willing to listen to my stories even when I couldn't get to the point. They didn't mind fragmented, interrupted, never-finish-a-complete-thought conversations, which for a few years pretty much defined my pattern of communication. My grown-up mommy girlfriends were happy just to be with me and my crew, whether they were helping clean old candy-bar wrappers from my car, size-six dresses from my closet, or grimy grout on my countertops. Somehow, doing the everyday stuff was fun with them by my side.

We used to show each other our tummy scars, trade more-information-than-anyone-needed-to-know labor stories, and help each other save money by giving each other salon treatments at home. They believed with me that mothers really do hold the world by the hand—child by child, day by day, prayer by prayer.

But perhaps their most magical gift was that my grown-up mommy girlfriends made me feel better when I didn't feel very grown-up at all.

Who are your "grown-up mommy girlfriends," and how do they encourage you? . . .

_____

_____

_____

_____

_____

_____

_____

_____

_____

_____

_____

_____

_____

_____

_____

A mother's generosity

CHAPTER TEN

Generosity

A mother's generosity guides her child to give.

For some people generosity comes easily. Others must work to remember our many blessings and the greater needs of those around us. It's always easier to take than to give, and most children are takers by nature.

How can we help them develop generous hearts? Sharing our love, our time, our concern—giving of ourselves—is the most powerful way we can help our children become givers.

Look into
your child's eyes
and say,
"Share your
blessings
with others."

Favorite Things

"I just can't believe it," I responded over the phone to my friend as I collected the cinnamon-toast crusts and juice cups from breakfast. My children were still in their pajamas and playing quietly in the den. "Was anyone hurt?" I asked as I sat down at the kitchen table. "Thank goodness," I sighed.

"Mommy," my four-year-old called as he came into the kitchen. "Where's my blankie?" I motioned him over and, holding the phone between my ear and shoulder, managed to hand him the blanket. He'd been toting that blanket around since he was born. It was always with him.

"I'd be glad to help. I have lots of extra kitchen items, and the kids have tons of clothes they don't even wear. I'll put a bunch of things together and buy whatever else is needed. Thanks for calling me." I felt so sad for my friend and her family. They had just lost their home and most of their belongings in a fire.

After explaining to my children about the fire and reassuring them that their friends were safe, I started gathering items and stacking them in piles in the living room. Glancing around my home at the antique sofa I loved, the floral curtains I had made, and the many framed photographs of our family, I felt sort of guilty. Guilty because I had so much and guilty because I was glad I hadn't lost my home.

Although I sincerely wanted to help my friend, it was really only an organizational chore for me. I didn't give her the shirt off my back or the food from my table. I'd probably never even miss the things I was collecting for her: the new coffeepot still in the box, the set of pots I had received when I opened a checking account, some hand towels I'd never used because they didn't quite match my décor. Most of the stuff I didn't even remember having until I began hunting around for items she needed. What would I have done if helping my friend had meant sacrificing my favorite things or supplies needed for myself or my family? I'd like to think I would have been just as anxious to help, but I wasn't sure.

The next morning I went to the living room to put the piles into boxes and take them to my friend. On the top of the stack of children's clothes was my son's blanket. I tossed it on the sofa and continued packing. He'd be panicked if I mistakenly gave away his blankie. I walked to the kitchen for more tape, and when I returned, the blanket was back at the top of the pile. "Sweetie, if you leave this blanket here, I might accidentally give it away," I called to my son. "Here, you hold on to it," I said as he joined me amid the piles.

"No, Mommy. I want to give my blanket to your friend. You're giving things, and I want to give something too."

"Are you sure?" I asked, pulling him up on my lap.

He nodded with solemn resolution. "It's the only thing I have that will make her feel better."

It wasn't the newest, but it was certainly the most precious gift in the box.

Write the story of a time your child gave a gift from the heart . . .

A mother gives her chi

CHAPTER ELEVEN

Honesty

A mother

gives her child

the strenght to

be honest.

$\mathcal{F}$ew things anger a mother more than a child who "tells a story." Yet it's so easy to compromise honesty. We usually think of dishonesty as overt lies—offensive behavior—when actually the dishonesty we encounter most often is subtle. It even stems from our desire to please others.

Our expectations of honesty will help our children to admit their wrongdoings and to stand firm against a world full of indiscretions.

Touch your
child's hand
reassuringly
and say, "Always
tell the truth, no
matter how afraid
you might be."

The Prize

In Mrs. Grady's kindergarten class, each child helped to monitor his or her own behavior by using the traffic-light system the teacher had developed. Below the chalkboard was a line of construction-paper traffic lights, one for each child. Green meant "You're behaving well," yellow, "You need some help controlling your actions," and red, "You're not being a good listener." Each child also had a paper circle with his or her name on it. On Fridays, the children whose circles had remained on green all week got to pick a little trinket from the prize box.

The first week, my son managed to keep a green light and chose a plastic spider from the prize box. I was proud of the little spider that represented good behavior, especially since my son was what teachers tactfully referred to as "high energy." I was sure the spider foretold greater things: honor roll, football trophies, job promotions.

My son earned quite a collection of these tokens, but on the fifth Friday, he left the school empty-handed and angry. He hadn't gotten to choose a reward from the box.

"Why didn't you get a prize?" I asked.

"Because I got a red light yesterday," he declared heatedly as he kicked a loose rock in the parking lot.

"Why did you get a red light?" The football trophies and job promotions seemed less certain.

"I didn't sit down when the teacher asked me to sit."

Maybe he could get a job that required standing. "Well, you have to listen to Mrs. Grady. Try to be a good listener next week, and then you can get a prize."

The next Friday afternoon, he ran out of the school with his fist tightly wrapped around a small yo-yo. "Look at this, Mom!" He held up the toy.

"Good job, honey," I said encouragingly. "I'm happy that you got a prize, but I'm even more happy that you listened to the teacher and behaved."

My son was quiet on the ride home from school. At dinner he wasn't eager to show the yo-yo to his father. That evening at bedtime, as I placed the yo-yo with his other prizes, he blurted out, "I don't like that yo-yo."

"Why not, honey? You earned it by listening to Mrs. Grady—you should be proud."

"But I didn't listen," he confessed.

"How did you get the yo-yo then?" I asked. "When Mrs. Grady wasn't looking, I moved my circle from red to green. She didn't see me," he replied guiltily.

"Oh," I said. Surely he was headed for tax evasion, embezzlement, and fraud. I thought for a few seconds about how to turn his life around. "What do you think we should do?" I asked.

"Mrs. Grady will be mad at me." He struggled with his resolution. "But I guess I should give it back."

"That's a good idea," I said. He looked relieved and scared at the same time. "Don't worry," I said as I gave him a reassuring kiss good night. "I'll go with you. We'll tell the truth together." Maybe he could still be president.

Tell the story of a time your child struggled with the truth . . .

_____

_____

_____

_____

_____

_____

_____

_____

_____

_____

_____

_____

_____

_____

_____

_____

_____

_____

A mother hopes fo

CHAPTER TWELVE

Hope

A mother

hopes for good

things to come.

Sometimes it seems nearly impossible to believe that after every storm there's a rainbow, to hope for a better tomorrow. The little troubles of motherly life—a crying child and a sink full of dishes—coupled with the greater concerns of marriage and money can leave us feeling discouraged.

That's when it takes the eye of hope to see the brilliant spectrum of color amid the clouds.

Rest your
child's head upon
your shoulder
and say, "Never
stop hoping."

Rainbow's End

My daughter was fascinated with rainbows. She lined up her crayons in rainbow order and selected clothes based on their rainbow appeal. When anyone asked her what her favorite color was, she would reply, "Rainbow." She drew colorless rainbows in the sand at the beach and chalk rainbows on the driveway at home.

"Why do you like rainbows so much?" I asked when she was five years old.

"There's always something special at the end of a rainbow," she replied.

"You mean like treasure?"

"All kinds of treasures—pretty pictures and nice words and hugs and kisses and candy and stuff like that. The stuff that makes you feel better when you're sad or hurt. Good stuff," she responded.

A few weeks later, my daughter had a seizure caused by a high fever. I felt helpless watching her small body convulse. The worst possibilities ran through my mind. I called 911, and an ambulance sped to the scene. After her active seizure stopped, my daughter remained unresponsive in an emergency-room bed. My hope that she would be OK faded with every passing hour in which we saw no improvement.

The local hospital was helpful and caring, but not equipped to deal with her neurological state. She would need to be transported by helicopter to the university medical center. Just as my husband and I signed the necessary papers and the staff prepared to move her, she awoke—groggy, but aware of her surroundings. She was going to be fine.

I climbed on the hospital bed and held her in my arms, rocking her back and forth like a small infant. She relaxed in the comfort of my arms. "Mommy"—she looked up at me—"Do you believe in rainbows?"

"Of course I do, honey," I said as I brushed the matted hair away from her eyes.

"When I was sick," she said dreamily, "I was sliding down the rainbow to get to you. Remember, I told you there's always something good at the end of a rainbow."

"You sure did, baby."

That summer after a terrific thunderstorm, two rainbows, not one, appeared across the lake behind our backyard. My husband spotted them first and called the children out onto the deck to see the spectacular sight. The scene was met with squeals of delight, admiring "Ahs," and quiet awe. My five-year-old tugged at my dress, trying to get my full attention. When I turned to her, she declared exuberantly, "Rainbows are real!" I looked at her quizzically. She'd always talked about rainbows. I had assumed she knew they were real.

When I tucked her into bed that night, I asked her about seeing the rainbows. "I thought you knew rainbows were real, sweetie."

"I saw pictures before," she said, "but I never saw a real one. I always just hoped in my heart that rainbows were real." Then she looked at me and giggled as if I were being silly. "You don't need to see something to hope."

"You're absolutely right, honey." I'd never let go of hope again.

How has your child renewed the hope in your heart? . . .

_____

_____

_____

_____

_____

_____

_____

_____

_____

_____

_____

_____

_____

_____

_____

_____

A mother knows joy

CHAPTER THIRTEEN

Joy

A mother

knows joy because

she has a child.

It's so easy to wish away our joyous times in search of happiness. "When my child is older, things will be better." "If my husband gets that job promotion, life will improve." Happiness is based on the circumstances around us, and no matter how organized or goal-oriented we mothers are, it's impossible to control everything.

True joy comes when we learn to accept life as it comes and appreciate its inherent beauty.

Touch your child's
cheek softly
and say,
"No one can ever
take the joy from
your heart."

Mud Puddles and Rain Boots

The whole family was looking forward to a break from routine. We had scheduled lots of activities for Memorial Day weekend—a picnic at the park, a visit to the 4-H fair, and horseback riding at a local farm. What we hadn't planned on were the torrential rains and the coolest May temperatures in forty years.

"Three days off from school!" my oldest shouted as he flung his backpack onto the kitchen counter.

"We're going to have so much fun," my daughter added. I was making their favorite meal, spaghetti and meatballs, and after dinner we would have a special movie night.

"What's up for tomorrow, Mom?" my other daughter asked.

"Horseback riding!" I announced, and they all cheered.

The rain started during dinner, and by the time we cleared the table, it was coming down heavily. But the worst of the storm was forecast to be over by tomorrow, so we were still optimistic about our plans.

Everyone stretched out on blankets on the den floor and was enjoying the show. It was a perfect family evening . . . and then the lights flickered. Then the lights went out. The children groaned, and my husband felt his way upstairs to gather some candles and matches. The darkness was a little unsettling at first, but with the glow of the candlelight, we relaxed again on our blankets. "Now what do we do?" one of the children asked.

"We talk and enjoy one another's company," I answered.

They responded with a collective sigh.

"Why don't we chat about places we'd like to travel?" I suggested. The conversation started slowly, but eventually we were dreaming of Dunn's River Falls in Jamaica, the Mediterranean Sea off the coast of Sicily, and the lake at my parents' house in North Carolina.

We drifted off to sleep and woke the next morning expecting working appliances. The power was still out. The kids thought it was great. For breakfast we ate hot dogs they roasted over a fire in the fireplace. Though we repeatedly tried to flip on lights, use the microwave, or turn on the radio, we were content to read, play board games, and just hang out. By afternoon we grabbed our boots and raincoats and went outside for a walk in the light drizzle. We jumped in puddles on the path in front of our home. Splashing was made into an art form with leaping and laughing.

At last we went inside to dry off. About the time we were lying on our blankets for another family chat, the power was restored. Much to my surprise, the children sighed in disappointment. "I thought you'd be happy when the lights came back on," I said.

"But now we'll have to go back to our old life," my oldest daughter lamented.

I realized we never really needed all those activities to have fun. We just had to stop long enough to appreciate the beauty of the world around us and the joy of love in our own family. Not exactly the vacation we had imagined, but it was just the vacation we needed.

Write about a time you found unexpected joy in undesirable circumstances . . .

_____

_____

_____

_____

_____

_____

_____

_____

_____

_____

_____

_____

_____

_____

A mother fills her

CHAPTER FOURTEEN

Laughter

A mother

fills her home

with laughter.

Some days the challenges of motherhood can reduce us to tears. Anxiety leads to sleepless nights. Yet when a child's grin turns into uninhibited, rolling laughter, we, too, find ourselves laughing in a way we had almost forgotten.

Children remind us to fill our homes with laughter—to laugh at the silliness of the world, at everyday discoveries—even at those little trials in our lives.

Smile adoringly
at your child
and say,
"Fill your life
with laughter."

Blue Jeans

Under the pretense of maternal cravings, I had put on quite a few extra pounds downing doughnuts and pizza throughout my fourth pregnancy. During my last trimester, friends would affectionately pat my bulging tummy and say, "You're all baby." Had that been true, I would have given birth to a forty-pound infant and left the maternity ward wearing my jeans. Instead I gave birth to a nine-pounder, which left me with . . . well, you can do the math.

With three daughters already at home, my husband and I had always tried to avoid using the word *diet*, preferring instead to use the phrase *healthy eating*. I must admit, we *said* healthy eating more than we actually *did* healthy eating.

Taking off the postpregnancy weight was more difficult than I had expected. When I was younger, I could eat anything and never gain a pound. Life caught up with me. So I decided on a weight-loss strategy: walk every morning, eat less sugar, and give up processed foods. In fact, I thought it was a good idea for the whole family.

Every morning after my walk, I would mark the calendar with a star to reflect my efforts. The one thing I didn't do was weigh myself. The fluctuation of a pound or two one way or the other wreaked havoc with my attitude. I decided to gauge my weight loss by how my clothes fit, blue jeans being the best indicator.

With a family of six, I did quite a bit of laundry, and during the early years, the children were too young to assist. But my husband pitched in from time to time, and unlike me, he even put the folded clothes in the dresser drawers. I usually left them stacked in a basket in our bedroom. I always meant to put them away, but somehow we ended up just fishing out what we needed from there.

It was my habit to dress the kids first and then throw on my clothes right before driving them to school. One morning I grabbed a pair of jeans from my dresser and put them on. To my surprise, they fit! In fact, they were a bit loose. I was thrilled. I threw on some makeup, fluffed my hair, and headed out to chauffeur my kids to school like I was going to the Oscars. The school drop-off area became my red carpet, and I hung out chatting with other moms like I was indulging the paparazzi. Life was good.

I cooked a special dinner for the family that night and pranced around the dining room in high heels and my sleek jeans, waiting for my husband to notice my leaner figure. I caught him staring at me as I got up to serve him another helping of vegetables. Then he asked.

"Are those my jeans you're wearing?"

Tell the story of the last really good laugh your family had together . . .

_____

_____

_____

_____

_____

_____

_____

_____

_____

_____

_____

_____

_____

_____

_____

A mother loves he

CHAPTER FIFTEEN

Love

A mother

loves her child

unconditionally.

As mothers it's easy to get frustrated and angry with our kids—especially when they make poor choices. But children don't always understand that moms can be angry and still love them.

Much like our children want to hear the same story over and over, even though they know the ending, they also need to hear "I love you" again and again.

Kiss your
child tenderly
and vow,
"I will always
love you."

The Spot on the Rug

"What's that on the rug?" I demanded in the irritated mommy voice that sends kids running. My daughter just stared at me, almost afraid to speak. When she did start to offer an explanation, I cut her off. "How many times have I told you not to bring paint into your room? Do you know how much carpet costs? You'd better hope that stain comes out!"

Her eyes began to well up with tears, and I knew she felt bad about spilling the paint, but I was angry. Contemplating the best way to extract red watercolor from a beige carpet, I headed downstairs for some cleaning products and towels.

When I returned to my daughter's room, she was rubbing the red spot with a ball of tissues. Now the carpet was flecked with little pieces of white. "That's OK, honey, I'll do that," I said as I moved in on the stain. "What a mess," I muttered. As I scrubbed, I explained to my daughter why she couldn't paint in her room—just in case it wasn't clear. "You can paint in the kitchen," I told her.

After dinner my daughter took a bath, brushed her teeth, and headed to her room for bed. "I'll be right there to tuck you in," I assured her. Even though she knew how to read, each night I read a portion of a chapter book to her. That night we laughed about the silly antics of the children in the story. I thought everything was fine.

I switched off her lamp, but we could still see by the light coming from the hall. As I leaned down to give her a hug and a kiss, she pulled out a white, construction-paper card from under her pillow. A giant, red heart was painted on the front. On the inside she had painted "I love you, Mommy." Now I knew why she had the paint in her room. At the bottom of the page, this time with a pen, she had drawn two squares—one with yes printed beside it and the other with a no. Above the boxes she had written the question: "Do you still love me?"

She offered me a pencil and waited for me to check off my answer. I filled the yes box with a big, affirmative check. My daughter smiled with relief. "I thought you didn't love me anymore because I spilled paint on the carpet and it made you angry."

I kissed her tenderly. "I will *always* love you. Even when I'm angry or upset, I still love you."

The paint never completely came out of the carpet, but I don't mind. The spot faded to a light pink that seems to me to resemble the vague shape of a heart. Now every time I go into my daughter's room, I'm reminded to tell her "I love you." No matter what.

Write about a time when your love overpowered your frustration with your child . . .

A mother slows her p

CHAPTER SIXTEEN

Patience

A mother slows her pace to match her child's.

121

$\mathcal{P}$atience is our ability to cope when things don't go as we planned. As mothers that would be most of the time. We're not perfect.

When things don't go our way, we sometimes get angry or frustrated, say things we don't mean, even act like a child ourselves. But part of being a mother is learning to step in time with our children—to just slow down and be patient.

Take your child's
hand in yours
and say,
"Be patient
with others."

Every Day

My plan was pretty simple. Not an architectural drawing for a skyscraper or financial goals for a major corporation. I just wanted to get my four kids dressed and fed. Then I wanted to get in the car without mishap and drop them off at school on time.

My plan almost always failed.

My kids seemed to think the definition of *hurry* was "Mommy's getting cranky." They each had their own plans, which changed from minute to minute.

One hopeful morning, my son was actually trying to follow my plan by putting on his shoes . . . except he couldn't find his shoes. My preschooler was tracing raindrops with her syrupy finger on the just-Windexed-yesterday window, and my other child was hanging out, watching the rush of the morning. The baby . . . well, she always needed a diaper change at the very time everyone was finally in the car and I had turned the key in the ignition. I think I could potty-train her with the sound of a starting car instead of the conventional running of water in the bathroom.

Anyway, as I sat there reconciling myself to the probability that we would again be late for school, I started muttering. "An engineer has it easier. You can bend steel, but try getting a diaper on a one-year-old with an arched back."

After dropping off the two school-age children, I headed to the grocery store with the baby and pre-schooler, optimistic that the morning could only get better. I daydreamed about a parking space right in front, plastic vegetable bags that open, no-wait deli counters, sales on Crystal Light and hair color, and a checkout person who is fast, friendly, and honors my just-expired coupons.

Here's what happened. I wheeled the cart with my smashed-banana-covered baby to the checkout line and loaded the conveyor belt with on-sale stuff. I fumbled for the coupons and grocery card the checkout person required before she would check me out. I told her we had eaten two bananas. The register tape ran out, the baby was pulling items off the display stand, and the clerk was trying to figure out how to weigh two bananas that weren't there, oblivious to the fact that I had someplace to go and had to get there quickly.

I noticed an older woman behind me with only a few items in her basket. "You may want to go to another line," I suggested apologetically.

"That's all right. My kids are all grown, and I have nowhere to rush off to. I'm just enjoying watching your lovely family," she replied with a smile.

It was at that moment that I started to understand patience. I was always charging off with my to-do list in hand, thinking that when everything was done, which it never was, I could enjoy life. I realized that what I was doing every day *was* life. Patience was my ability to step in time with my children amid the everyday stuff a mommy does.

I still had to get my kids off to school, but when I just slowed down and loved the life I was in, I found my patience.

Tell the story of a time you slowed your pace to match your child's . . .

_____

_____

_____

_____

_____

_____

_____

_____

_____

_____

_____

_____

_____

_____

_____

_____

_____

A mother knows

CHAPTER SEVENTEEN

Prayer

A mother knows God answers prayer.

With the precious bundle of a child in our arms, it's easy to think the responsibility for our kids rests entirely in our hands. It is the job of mothers to feed, teach, and love them. But our children are also God's children, and He provides support and love in raising them. That support and love extend to us as mothers too.

After all, we're His children. And when we talk to Him, He listens.

*Fold your child's
hands in prayer
and say,
"Ask God for help."*

Tickets

I used to think prayers were like a long strand of carnival tickets. You only got so many, and once you used them, they were gone. When I became a mother, I realized I needed every prayer ticket I could find—and more.

My teenage son had been ill for many months. The countless physicians we had called upon could not diagnose what was wrong with him. I was the one who first noticed how his left shoulder had begun to droop. He complained of a sore throat often, and he had trouble hearing. A test for Lyme disease was negative. He didn't have strep or mononucleosis. He was clearly not well, but no one could figure out why.

Finally an MRI showed a tumor the size of a golf ball at the base of his skull behind his left ear. The pressure of the tumor on a series of nerves was causing muscle deterioration in his shoulder, declining vocal coordination that resulted in a sore throat, and what could be complete loss of hearing in his left ear. He needed surgery immediately.

My husband and I were afraid our son would lose his

hearing or even that we might lose our son. My son was more concerned about shaving his head for the procedure and the scar his surgery might leave behind.

I had prayed for my son through bumps and bruises, scrapes and sprains, chicken pox and car crashes. I prayed for him during the initial search for a diagnosis and throughout the pursuit of treatment, but this time God seemed distant. Where was the healing? Had I run out of tickets?

In the hospital, sitting with my son, I tried to convey confidence. "You're going to be fine, honey," I reassured him. "Every night since you were a baby, I've asked God to watch over you and keep you safe. Then I would recite to you a little poem about God's angels. When you were too old to want to hear it, I'd go back in your room long after you were asleep and say it anyway. I would pray, 'God, please watch over my beautiful child. Let the rain in his life be gentle, the wind be soft at his back, and his path be clear. May Your angels meet him at every turn.'"

"Do you really think God hears our prayers, Mom?"

"I sure do, sweetie." There was a pause.

"Then why didn't He answer you? You've been praying for me to get better, but I haven't."

I'd struggled with that for months, yet suddenly the answer became crystal clear. God had heard my prayers, and He was working a solution. "I think my prayers *are* being answered," I said. "You're going to be better as soon as you have this operation."

After more than ten hours of microscopic surgery to remove the entangled tumor from the strand of nerve cells, my son was fine. I could feel God and His angels surrounding us that day, taking care of my son—and me.

Now I know prayer is more like a carnival wristband. You can ride as many times as you like.

Write your own story of answered prayer . . .

_____

_____

_____

_____

_____

_____

_____

_____

_____

_____

_____

_____

_____

_____

_____

_____

_____

_____

THE Motherhood CLUB
Making a Difference One Kiss at a Time

mc

...born from a simple idea: *honor Mom for doing the most important job in the world.*

Titles included in THE Motherhood CLUB™:

Prayer Guide: *The Busy Mom's Guide to Prayer*
—Lisa Whelchel

Parenting: *Mom-PhD*
—Teresa Bell Kindred

There's a Perfect Little Angel in Every Chil
—Gigi Schweikert

Inspiration: *The Miracle in a Mother's Hug*
—Helen Burns

Gift: *Holding the World by the Hand*
—Gigi Schweikert

Fiction: *Tight Squeeze*
—Debbie DiGiovanni

Devotional: *"I'm a Good Moth*
—Gigi Schweikert

"At The Motherhood Club, you'll find bo to meet all your mothering needs."
—Lisa Whelchel
(From The Facts of